Happy Birthday!
from
Stamford Central School

ToMaria

To Dear Jen
With Love from
Maria W./mom— Her

Crabapples

Ballet School

Bobbie Kalman & Petrina Gentile
Photographs by Marc Crabtree

Crabtree Publishing Company

Crabapples

created by bobbie kalman

for Petrina and Marc, who worked so hard on this book

Editor-in-Chief
Bobbie Kalman

Writing team
Bobbie Kalman
Petrina Gentile

Managing editor
Lynda Hale

Editors
Tammy Everts
David Schimpky

Computer design
Lynda Hale
David Schimpky

Color separations and film
Dot 'n Line Image Inc.

Printer
Worzalla Publishing Company

Special thanks to
The staff and students of the National Ballet School, especially Stephen Johnson, Mavis Staines, Carole Chadwick, Mora Oxley, Lindsay Melcher, Leslie Scott, Janet Winger, Chris Zielinski, Stephanie Vanneste, Sofia Colaiacovo, Tamara Jones, Nicole Papadopoulos, Shaun Chandra-Geji, and Sebastian Stewart; and the National Ballet of Canada

Illustrations
Halina Below-Spada: page 22
Antoinette "Cookie" DeBiasi: pages 9, 10, 13, 27 (both)
Lisa Smith: page 23

Photographs
All photographs taken by Marc Crabtree, except for the following:
Mike Conley/The Standard: pages 6 (both), 7 (both)
B. Gray/The National Ballet of Canada: pages 4, 28, 29 (both)
The National Ballet of Canada: page 32

For more information about the National Ballet School, contact:
Registrar's Office
105 Maitland Street
Toronto, Ontario
Canada, M4Y 1E4

Crabtree Publishing Company

350 Fifth Avenue
Suite 3308
New York
N.Y. 10118

360 York Road, RR 4
Niagara-on-the-Lake
Ontario, Canada
L0S 1J0

73 Lime Walk
Headington
Oxford OX3 7AD
United Kingdom

Cataloging in Publication Data
Kalman, Bobbie, 1947-
   Ballet school

(Crabapples)
Includes index.

ISBN 0-86505-606-4 (library bound)   ISBN 0-86505-706-0 (pbk.)
This book looks at the daily life and routine of students at a ballet school.

1. Ballet School. 2. Ballet dancing - Juvenile literature.
3. Ballet - Juvenile literature. I. Gentile, Petrina, 1969-   .
II. Title. III. Series: Kalman, Bobbie, 1947-   . Crabapples.

GV1788.6.N37K3 1994   j792.8'071'0713541   LC 94-35079
                                                          CIP

What is in this book?

Beautiful ballet!

A ballet performance is an amazing sight! Dancers dressed in colorful costumes tiptoe and leap across the stage. Their bodies seem to become one with the music, whether it is lively or sad.

Have you ever wondered how ballet
dancers learn to dance? It is not easy!
They work very hard for many years.
Some begin their training at the National
Ballet School of Canada. It is one of the
best ballet schools in the world!

Calling #8!

Each year, over 1000 young dancers audition to go to this school. The auditions are held in cities across Canada. Children who live far away audition by sending videotapes.

During the audition, the children take part in a 90 minute ballet class. They do stretches, jumps, and turns.

Teachers from the ballet school judge each dancer. The judges look for children who would become excellent dancers with the right training.

Student #1 was one of the lucky 150 students who were invited to be part of another audition at the ballet school. There she will be tested on both her ballet skills and school work. Will she be one of the 45 students to join the ballet school in September?

Moving in

Can you imagine leaving home and living at a new school? Many ballet school students must move into **residence** because their homes are too far away.

About 100 boys and girls live in residence, and up to four students share one bedroom. Children can choose their own roommates and change them throughout the year. The students share living rooms, lounges, bathrooms, telephones, and a cafeteria.

The girl in the top picture can't wait to get settled. Her mother is happy that she is going to such a fine school, but her family will miss her!

Being away from home can be difficult, but there are many people to help the students adjust. Each week, the students meet with **counselors** who advise them on how to deal with their busy schedule.

Chaperones take students shopping or to theater performances. Young students are also paired up with older students who become special friends to their little "brothers" or "sisters."

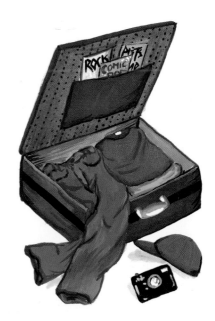

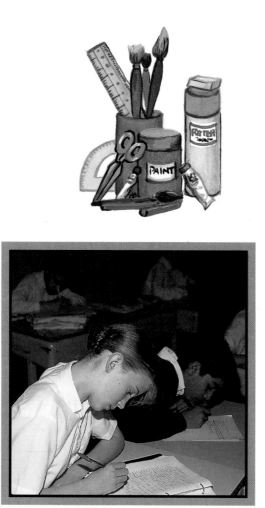

A school day

Ballet school students have a very long day. They begin school at 8:30 and often do not finish classes until 6:30 in the evening!

Each day the students study regular school subjects such as history and math. They have at least three hours of dance classes as well—even on Saturdays! The students also exercise in the pool to strengthen their muscles.

The students who live in residence have a two-hour homework period in the evening. A **tutor** visits them on school nights. He or she gives them additional help with their school work. Most of the students at the ballet school get very high grades.

Not only are the school days long, but so is the school year! Students in the sixth grade and up attend school until the end of July. They get only a month off!

In the classroom

The 150 students at the ballet school range from the fifth to the twelfth grade. Most classes have fewer than 20 students.

Students take a variety of subjects, including photography, music, art, French, chemistry, and computer science. They also study the history of ballet.

There are many regular classrooms at the ballet school, but the students are also taught in the film lab, music room, theater-arts studio, and library.

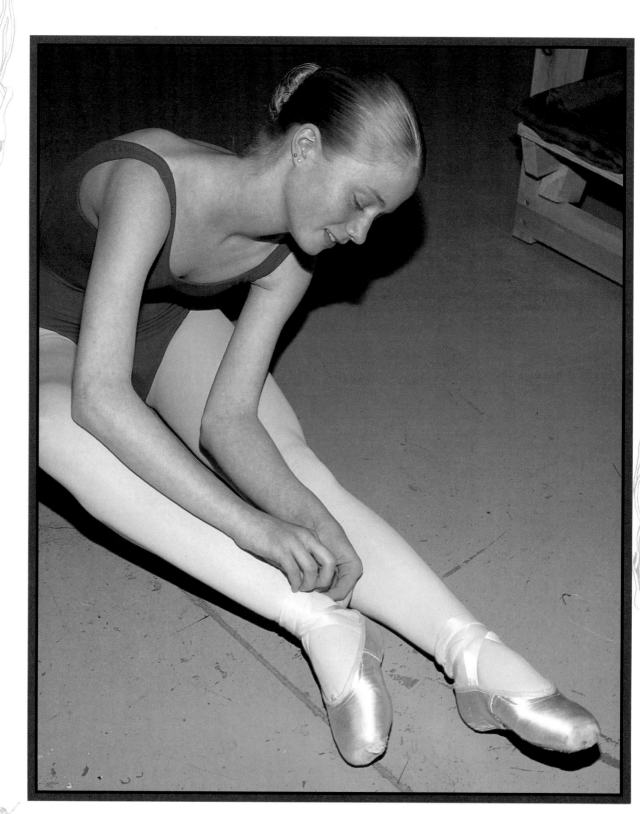

Dance dress

Students wear a **body suit**, or leotard, to dance class. Body suits allow dancers to move freely. They also allow teachers to see the exact body positions of the dancers.

On their feet, the girls wear soft slippers or **pointe** shoes. Pointe shoes help them stand on the tips of their toes. The young dancers learn to tie the ribbons of their pointe shoes neatly around their ankles.

The girls wear their hair in a tight bun. The older students teach the younger ones how to roll their hair up and pin it at the right spot. Loose hair can get in the way of a dancer's performance.

In the studio

Each dance class begins with **barre** exercises. A wooden bar helps the students keep their balance.

At the center, children repeat the barre moves without any support. They do jumps, stretches, turns, balances, and graceful back bends.

The class at the top practices the *battement tendu devant*, which means "leg stretched in front." Ballet terms are given in French because French is the language of ballet. Students perform the *battement tendu devant* exercise nearly 100 times in each class. Practice makes perfect!

Body moves

The students learn a variety of ballet positions in each grade. The boy on the left is standing with his feet in **fifth position**. The heel of his foot is placed against the toe of his other foot.

The boys below stand in the *cou-de-pied position devant*. The left toe is pointed down and touching the ankle of the other foot.

The girls are starting their class with **pointe exercises** at the barre. These exercises strengthen a dancer's legs.

In the center, the girls practice jumps. They must keep their backs straight and their arms in a curved position.

That smarts!

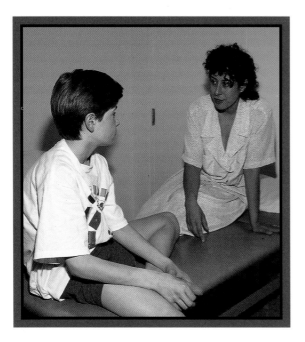

From time to time, dancers have injuries. When injuries occur, students visit a **physiotherapist**. There are two at the ballet school.

Physiotherapists treat muscle injuries with heat, exercises, and massage. They also teach students how to prevent injury by paying attention to pain or swelling in their legs.

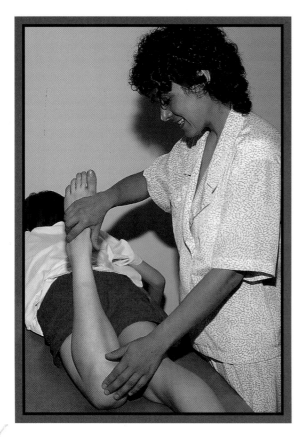

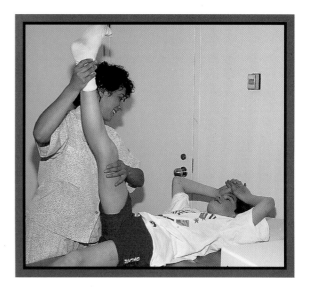

When children grow too quickly, they sometimes get muscle pain. The physiotherapist on the opposite page tests the length of a boy's muscles. She checks for swelling in his knee. She advises the young dancer to do more stretching exercises.

This young girl has knee pain. The physiotherapist attaches a machine to her leg. Electric currents from the machine will strengthen her muscles and help reduce the pain.

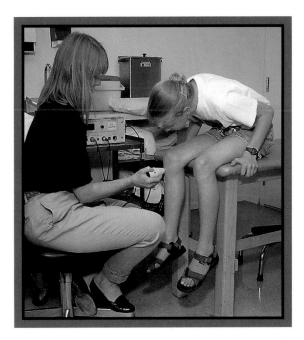

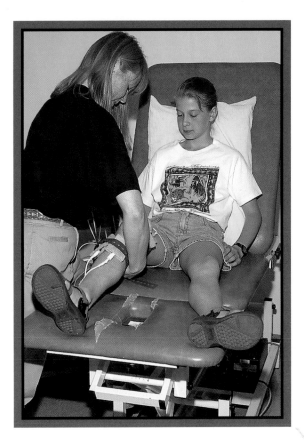

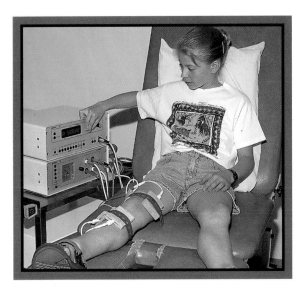

Food and nutrition

It is very important for young dancers to eat well. They need lots of energy. Proper foods provide that energy.

The **nutritionist** works with the chef to plan the meals at the ballet school. A nutritionist is a person who knows how to combine foods in a healthy way. She meets with the children to teach them good eating habits.

The chef prepares all the meals at the school. According to the students, his best meal is spaghetti with meat sauce, garlic bread, salad, and banana cake.

The chef is more than just a cook. He is a friend. He makes meals fun by using recipes that the children give him. He offers cooking classes to the older students. During the holidays, he prepares special meals for the students who live too far away to go home.

Time to relax

Ballet school students are just like other kids—they like to have fun. They play games, listen to music, read, or watch television. On the weekends they have time to relax from their busy schedule.

Some students take part in other school activities. They put on plays and performances. Sometimes they go to baseball games, shopping malls, the movies, or the zoo.

Ready for the show

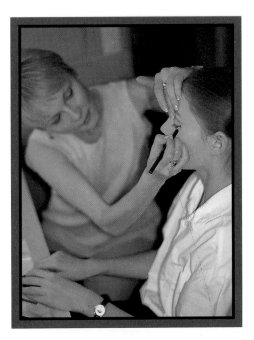

Ballet school students take part in many performances. Each year, they dance in a one-week Spring Showcase. Some students travel and perform around the world with the National Ballet of Canada.

The dressing room at the school is filled with costumes, headdresses, and wigs. Some are made by a costume maker at the school. This girl is wearing a costume from a famous ballet called the *Nutcracker*.

A makeup artist visits the ballet school and teaches girls how to put on their makeup. It can take up to 30 minutes to apply the makeup for a performance!

Time to perform!

Each year at Christmas time, a few lucky ballet school students are chosen to be part of a very special performance. They dance in a ballet called the *Nutcracker*, which is performed by the National Ballet of Canada. Thousands of people buy tickets to see this Christmas favorite.

The students who take part in the show practice their dancing almost every day. On the night of the show, they are rewarded for all their hard work with thunderous applause!

29

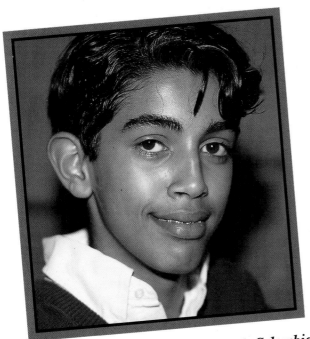

Wise words

Question: What advice would you give students who are interested in attending the National Ballet School?

Shaun, grade 7, Vancouver, British Columbia
"It's a lot harder than regular school because you have ballet and academic classes every day."

Nicole, grade 6, Edmonton, Alberta
"Expect more than you think, because it's really hard, but it's lots of fun!"

Sofia, grade 6, Ottawa, Ontario
"I want to become a dancer, and the training here is the best!"

Words to know

barre A wooden bar that helps dancers keep their balance
chaperone An adult who supervises young people
counselor A person who gives advice
nutritionist A person who knows how to combine foods in a healthy way
physiotherapist A person who treats injuries with heat, exercises, or massage

pointe exercises Exercises that dancers do while wearing their pointe shoes
pointe shoes Shoes that help dancers stand on the tips of their toes
residence A building with many bedrooms
tutor A person who gives students extra help with their homework

Index

The National Ballet School

In 1959, Betty Oliphant and Celia Franca started the National Ballet School—the first of its kind in North America. Located in Toronto, Canada, the school is known for its superb dance training and enriched academic program.

Since 1959, the number of students has increased from 27 to 150! Over one-third of the students are boys. The dance program, too, has changed. In addition to ballet, the students study modern dance.

The National Ballet School is ranked as one of the top ballet schools in the world. Its graduates include Karen Kain, Frank Augustyn, Veronica Tennant, Mavis Staines—the current Artistic Director of the National Ballet School—and most of the National Ballet of Canada dancers.

4 5 6 7 8 9 0   Printed in USA   3 2 1 0 9 8